WHS

NATIONAL TESTS
practice papers

FOR THE YEAR 2005

Optional Tests
Maths and English
Levels 2–5

practice papers

AGE
9–10
Year 5

Acknowledgements

The Publishers would like to thank the following for permission to reproduce copyright material:

Egil's Saga, adapted from texts by Magnus Magnusson
"A Liking for the Viking" by Celia Warren, taken from *Vikings Don't Wear Pants* by Roger Stevens and Celia Warren (King's England Press, 2001) in the *Potty Poets* series; see www.pottypoets.com
The Jorvic Viking Centre, adapted from the Jorvic Viking Centre website

Every effort has been made to trace all copyright holders, but if any have been inadvertently overlooked, the Publishers will be pleased to make the necessary arrangements at the first opportunity.

First published in 2005
exclusively for WHSmith by
Hodder Murray,
a member of the Hodder Headline Group
338 Euston Road
London NW1 3BH

Authors: Steve Mills and Hilary Koll (Maths); Christine Moorcroft and Ray Barker (English)

Impression 5 4 3 2 1
Year 2006 2005

Printed and bound in Spain

A catalogue record for this title is available from the British Library

ISBN 0 340 88870 9

NOTE: The tests, questions and advice in this book are not reproductions of the official test materials sent to schools. The official testing process is supported by guidance and training for teachers in setting and marking tests and interpreting the results. The results achieved in the tests in this book may not be the same as are achieved in the official tests.

Contents

Introduction

The National Tests: A Summary

What are the National Tests?

Children who attend state schools in England and Wales sit National Tests (also known as SATs) at the ages of 7, 11 and 14. Those at ages 11 and 14 are taken at the beginning of May. Those at age 7 can be carried out at any point during the year, as chosen by the teacher. Children in Wales may take the same tests at 11 and 14. All children may also sit optional tests in the intervening years – many schools have chosen to adopt these tests.

The results are used by the school to assess each child's level of knowledge and progress in English and Maths at Key Stage 1 and English, Maths and Science at Key Stages 2 and 3. They also provide useful guidance for the child's next teacher when he or she is planning the year's work.

The educational calendar for children aged 5–14 is structured as follows:

Key Stage	Year	Age by end of year	National Test
1 (KS1)	1	6	
	2	7	KEY STAGE 1
2 (KS2)	3	8	Optional Year 3
	4	9	Optional Year 4
	5	10	Optional Year 5
	6	11	KEY STAGE 2
3 (KS3)	7	12	Optional Year 7
	8	13	Optional Year 8
	9	14	KEY STAGE 3

Test timetable

The Key Stage 1 National Tests have so far been carried out in May but, from the school year beginning September 2004, teachers will be allowed greater flexibility as to when they test the children and which tests for tasks they use. Key Stage 1 tests are now based on teacher assessment and can take place at any point during the year as chosen by the teacher.

Key Stage 2 tests take place in one week in May. All children sit the same test at the same time. In 2005, the tests will take place in the week of **9–13 May**. Your child's school will be able to provide you with a detailed timetable.

Key Stage 3 students will sit their tests on **3–6 May**.

Levels

National average levels have been set for children's results in the National Tests. The levels are as follows:

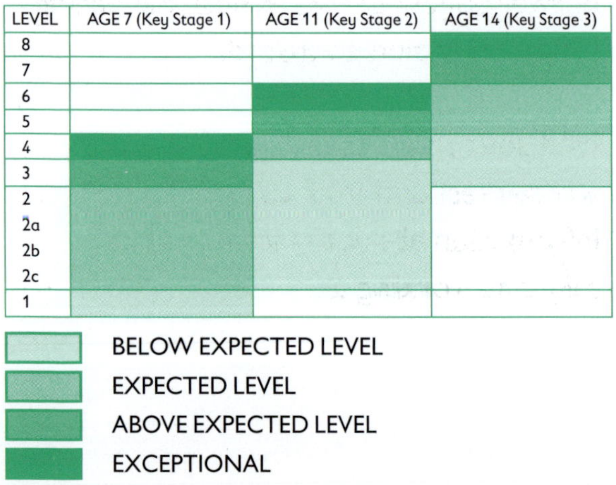

Results

Your child's school will send you a report indicating his or her levels in the tests and the teacher assessment.

The school's overall test results will be included in local and national league tables, which are published in most newspapers.

What can parents do to help?

While it is never a good idea to encourage cramming, you can help your child to succeed by:

- making sure he or she has enough food, sleep and leisure time during the test period
- practising important skills such as writing and reading stories, spelling and mental maths
- telling him or her what to expect in the test, such as important symbols and key words
- helping him or her to be comfortable in test conditions including working within a time limit, reading questions carefully and understanding different ways of answering.

Maths at Year 5

Typical seven-year-olds attain Level 2 in Maths at the end of Year 2. By the end of Year 5 most children will be working towards Level 4. Some might attain Level 5.

Setting the test

The written test

The written test is split into two parts, A and B. If your child scores highly in Part A, he or she can go on to try the harder questions in Part B. There is not a strict time limit on this test, but do not force your child to continue if he or she can no longer answer any questions.

Allow between 45 minutes and one hour to complete the written test. If your child attempts Part B, allow longer.

Your child will need a ruler, pencil, eraser and, if possible, a small mirror or piece of tracing paper. No extra writing paper is needed. Calculators should *not* be used.

If your child has difficulty in reading the questions, these can be read aloud, provided the mathematical words are not altered or explained. Where necessary, children can dictate their answers for you to write them down. For large numbers, however, a child should be clear which digits are intended to be written, e.g. for a number such as three thousand and six, the child must indicate that this should be written three, zero, zero, six.

The mental test

The marks scored on the Mental Maths Test are not included when levelling at Year 5. However, in the Year 6 National Test your child's mental scores will form part of the overall mark used for levelling.

The mental test should take approximately 10–15 minutes to give, and it is necessary for you to read aloud the questions on page 19, which you could copy for this purpose. Your child will only need a pencil and an eraser for the mental test.

The mental test contains a series of questions for you to read to your child and answer sheets for him or her to write answers on. Allow only the time suggested for each question and read each question twice.

Marking the test

Next to each question is a number indicating how many marks the question or part of the question is worth. Enter your child's mark into the circle, using the answer pages (22–26) to help you decide how many points to award.

Find your child's total score from the written test and refer to page 27 for information about the level your child might be working at.

Maths Test

Part A

1

1 Use all of these digits to make a **three-digit number smaller than 390**.

3	4	9

Write the number you have made in words.

three hundred and forty nine.

1

2 The **sum** of the digits of **one** of these telephone numbers is **27**. Whose number is it?

Theresa
020 7456 7243

Ling
07990 174593

Jackie
01941 352 5311

Ingrid
0117 2525112

Ingrid

TOTAL

2

3 Draw a line to join each answer to the matching question.

26	68 + 14
42	14 x 3
57	6 x 6
36	100 – 74
82	(20 x 3) – 1
59	28 + 29

2

4 Fill in the missing numbers in these sequences.

a 1, 4, 9, 16, 25, 36

1

b 3, 6, 12, 24, 48, 96

1

TOTAL

4

5 This is a diagram to show the number of children who have pets in Class 5.

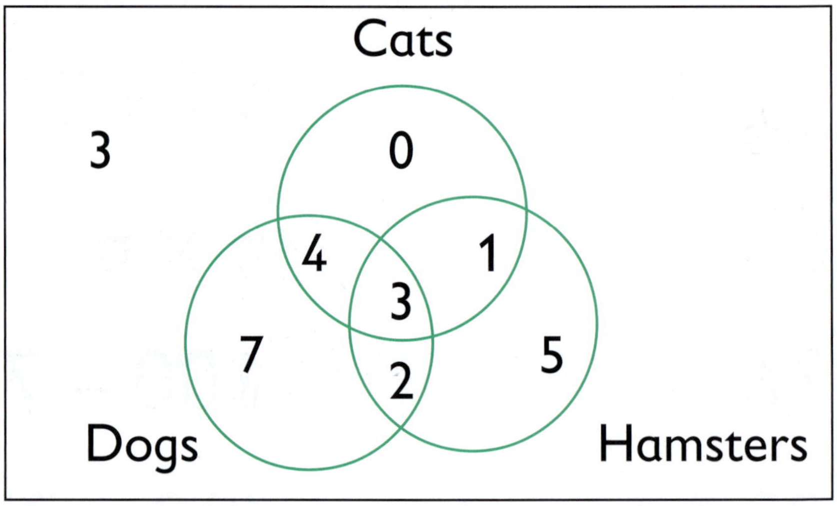

a How many children have a cat **and** a dog but no hamster?

4 children

1

b How many children have **only** a hamster?

5 children

1

c How many children do **not** have a cat, a dog or a hamster?

3 children

1

6 Finish this sentence.

A 2D shape with eight straight sides is called a

Octagon

1

TOTAL

4

7 Draw **all** the **lines of symmetry** onto each of the badges below. You can use a mirror or tracing paper.

2

Badge A

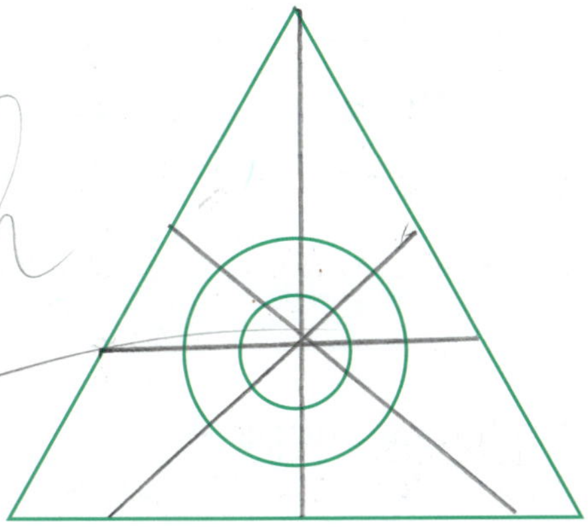

Badge B

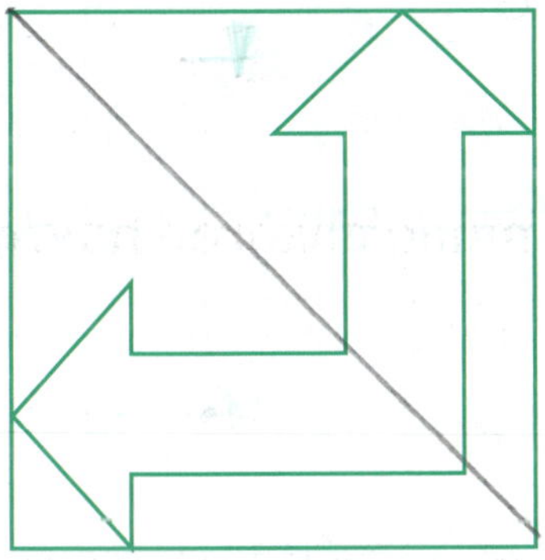

Badge C

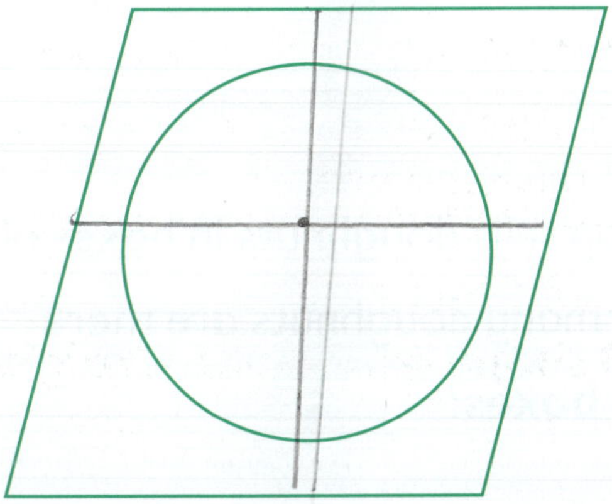

TOTAL

2

1

8 Draw a ring around **all** the numbers that when divided by **5** have a **remainder of 3**.

11 25 23 26

32 47 14 18

1

9 Find the area of Shape A.

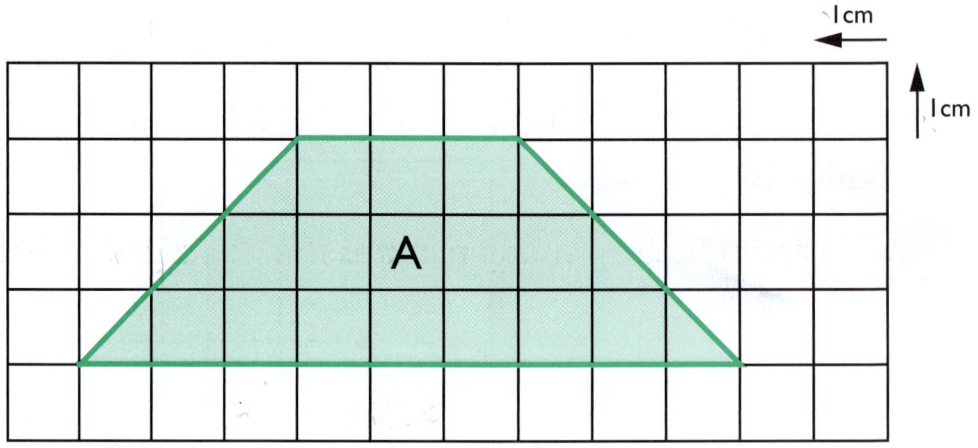

Area of Shape A = 18 cm^2

1

10 A shop sells doughnuts in boxes of four.

How many doughnuts are there in **64 boxes**?

256

TOTAL

3

11 This graph shows the journeys a lift made during half an hour. The lift travelled from the ground floor up to floor 7.

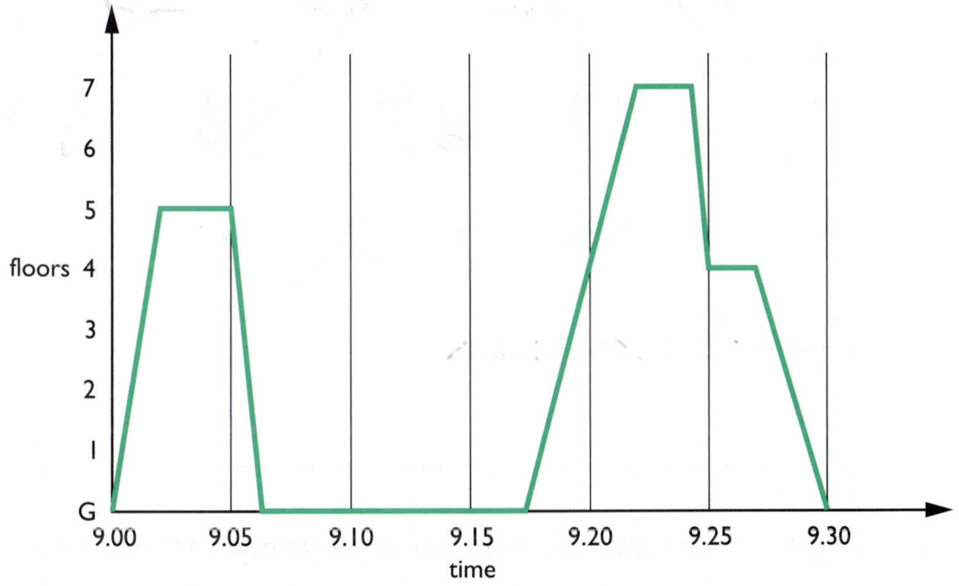

a Estimate how many minutes the lift stayed at floor 5.

3 minutes

1

b Where was the lift at 9.26?

Floor 4

1

c Estimate the time (to the nearest minute) that the lift reached floor 7.

9.22

1

TOTAL

3

12 Tick the picture below that is **not** a picture of a type of prism.

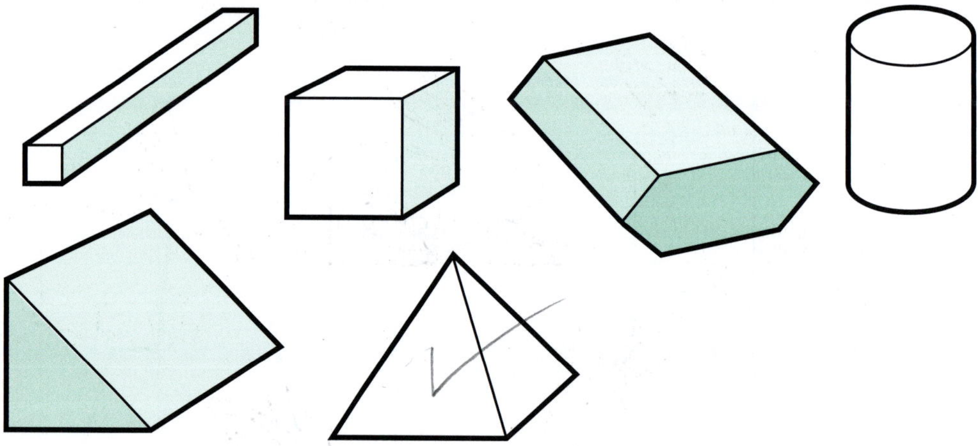

1

13 In your own words, explain what a square number is.

Well you use squre number when your using number's or dot's But I use number's. Such as ...

1

14 Fill in the missing numbers in the circles.

a 74 − (46) = 28

1

b (17) + 39 = 56

1

TOTAL

3

4

15 What fraction of this group of rabbits is grey?

$\frac{2}{5}$

1

16 Draw a tick inside the shape that has **more than three sides**, **reflective symmetry** and **one right angle**.

1

TOTAL

2

1

17 Sean has exactly **£2.65** in **5p** coins in his money box.

How many 5p coins does he have?

53

1

18 This kettle has a capacity of 2 litres. The ball indicates how much water is in the kettle.

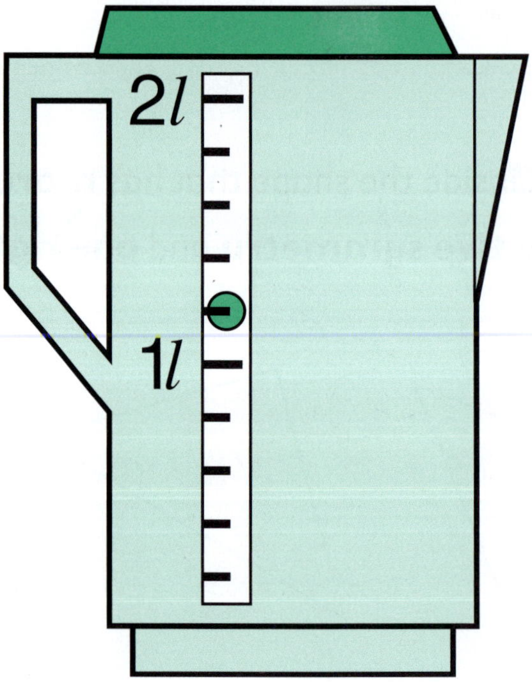

How many more millilitres of water would it take to fill the kettle to the 2 litre mark?

800 ml

TOTAL

2

19 Draw arrows to complete this diagram.

The arrows stand for:

→

"rounded to the nearest whole number is..."

6.9	**5**
6.21	
$5\frac{1}{4}$	**6**
$7\frac{7}{8}$	
6.09	**7**
7.48	
$5\frac{9}{10}$	**8**

2

TOTAL

2

20 When this spinner is spun, the probability of it landing on the number 1 is **one-half**. The probability of it landing on the number 2 is also **one-half**.

The spinner is spun a **first time** and lands on the number **2**. It is now spun a **second time**.

Put a cross on the line to show the probability of the spinner landing on the number **2** on the **second spin**.

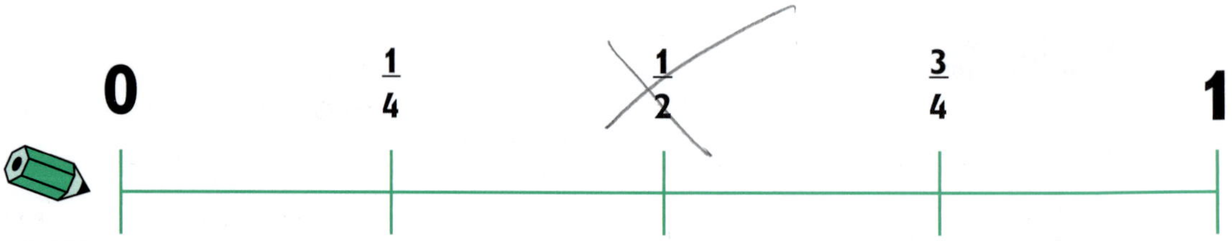

1

TOTAL

1

21 This triangle has
a perimeter of 30 cm.

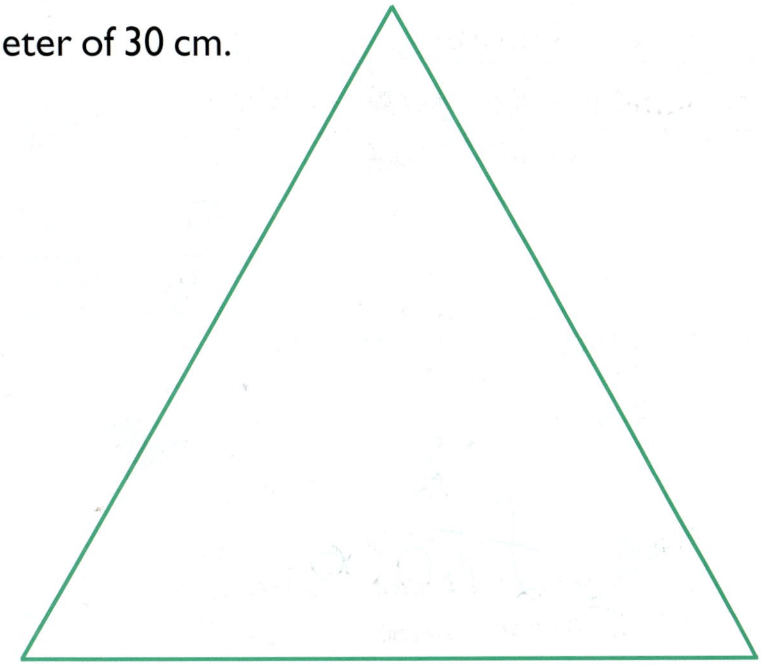

Use a ruler to draw a rectangle with a perimeter of 44 cm.

22cm

1

TOTAL

1

STOP HERE AND MARK THE TEST

Maths Test

Part B

22 Mr Smith works for "The Fix-it Firm".

He earns exactly **£500 per month**.

a How much does he earn in **one year**?

1

£6000

b The firm gives him a pay rise. He now earns **15%** more.

How much does he now earn **each month**?

1

£579

23 These prices were scanned into a shop till.

£5.63 £4.65 £8.98

£10.10 £9.07

Find the total of these prices.

1

£38.43

TOTAL

2

3

24 Zahir counts the number of times he can kick a ball in the air without it falling to the ground. He has tried this seven times.

These are his results:

12, 16, 11, 17, 20, 3, 20

What is the **median** of these numbers?

1

25 In a pack of number cards there are **10** cards numbered from 1 to 10. One card is picked at random.

Circle the fraction that shows the probability of it being a number **greater than 2**.

$\frac{1}{10}$ $\frac{4}{5}$ $\frac{5}{10}$ $\frac{10}{1}$ $\frac{6}{5}$ $\frac{4}{10}$

1

TOTAL

2

26 Here are some models, made from centimetre cubes, which form a pattern.

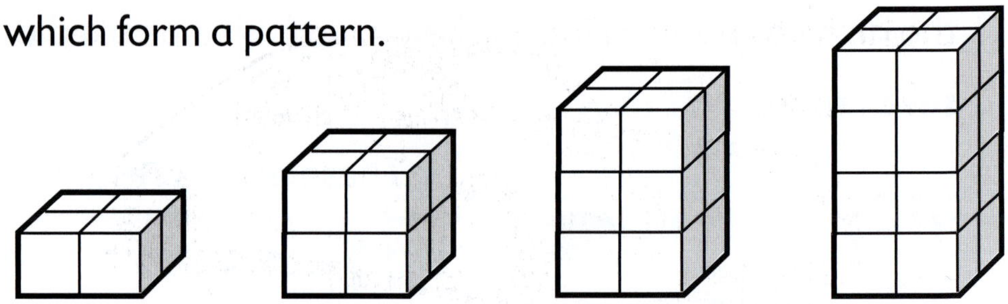

The relationship between the number of cubes and the height of the model can be written as:

the height of the model = the number of cubes ÷ 4

How many cubes are there in a model which has a height of 12 cm?

48 cubes

1

27 What numbers are the arrows pointing to?

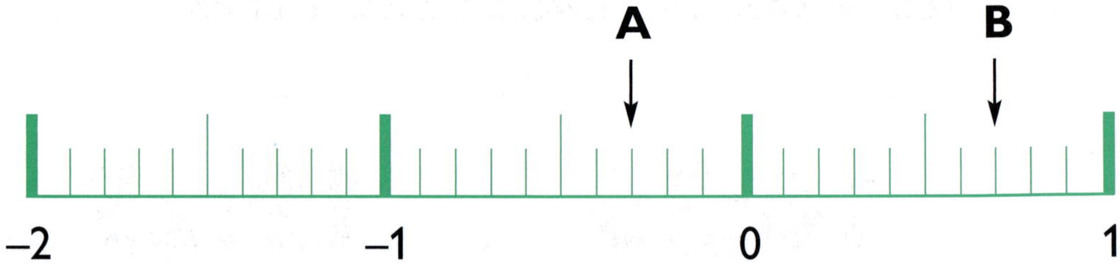

a A = -0.3

b B = 0.7

1

1

TOTAL

3

28 A car uses approximately **one litre** of petrol to travel **eight miles**.

a About how many litres of petrol does it use to travel **72 miles**?

9 litres

1

b Peter went on a journey in this car. He used **13 litres** of petrol. How many miles did he travel?

104 miles

1

29 Javed watched TV between these two times.

16:35	19:25

For how long did he watch TV?

2 hours	50 minutes

1

TOTAL

3

30 Charlotte goes on a **three kilometre** run.

Each pace she takes is **60 cm**.

How many paces does she take?

5000

1

31 $5x - 2 =$ ▲

If x is 3, what is the value of the triangle?

14

1

32 Fill in the missing numbers.

a $36.74 \div 100 =$ ◯

1

b $58.6 - 4.52 =$ ◯

1

TOTAL

1

4

STOP HERE AND MARK THE TEST

"For this first set of questions you have five seconds to work out each answer and write it down."

1 What is half of one hundred and four?

2 What is seven multiplied by eight?

3 Write the number six thousand and nine in figures.

4 What is fifty per cent of 60 kg?

5 A train journey begins at two thirty-five. It ends at three fifteen. How long does the journey last?

6 There are one hundred and twelve marbles in a jar. Seventy-five are red and the rest are blue. How many are blue?

7 Add seven and a half metres to three and a half metres.

8 What is ten more than one thousand one hundred and ninety five?

9 The temperature was six degrees and is now minus three degrees. By how much has the temperature fallen?

10 Look at the answer sheet. Which number is the arrow pointing to?

11 Six children share three pounds equally between them. How much does each child get?

12 Write two numbers that add up to seven and a half.

"For the next set of questions you have ten seconds to work out each answer and write it down."

13 How many grams are there in one and a half kilograms?

14 Look at the answer sheet. What is the median of these numbers?

15 What is the probability of rolling an even number on an ordinary dice?

16 What is the cost of five T-shirts at three pounds ninety-nine pence each?

17 What number is half-way between three point four and three point five?

18 Look at the drawing on the answer sheet. What will the shape look like when it is reflected in the mirror line? Shade the correct shape.

19 I'm thinking of a number. I double it and then subtract two. My answer is thirty. What is my number?

20 A clock shows eleven o'clock. What is the angle between the two hands?

Mental Maths Test

Answer Sheets

Five-second questions

1		
2		
3		
4	kg	50% 60 kg
5	minutes	2:35 3:15
6		112 75 red
7	metres	
8		
9	degrees	
10		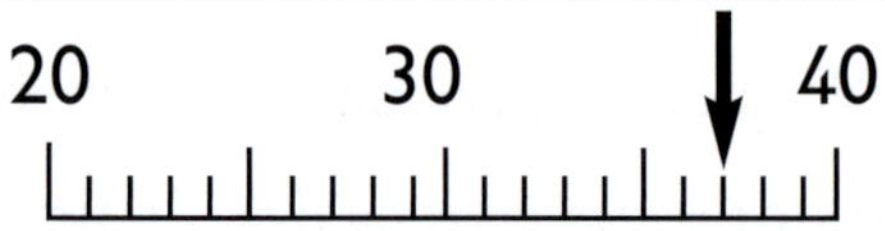
11	pence	
12		

1 1 1 1 1 1 1 1 1 1 1 1

TOTAL

12

Ten-second questions

13 ______ grams — 1

14 ______ | 6 8 / 8 / 3 5 — 1

15 ______ — 1

16 £ ______ | 5 £3.99 — 1

17 ______ — 1

18

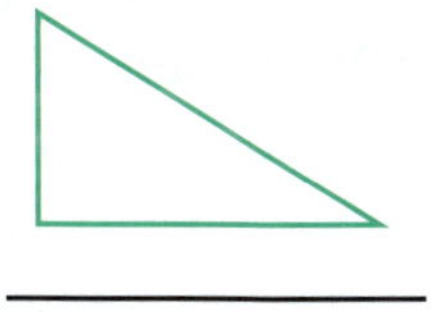

mirror line

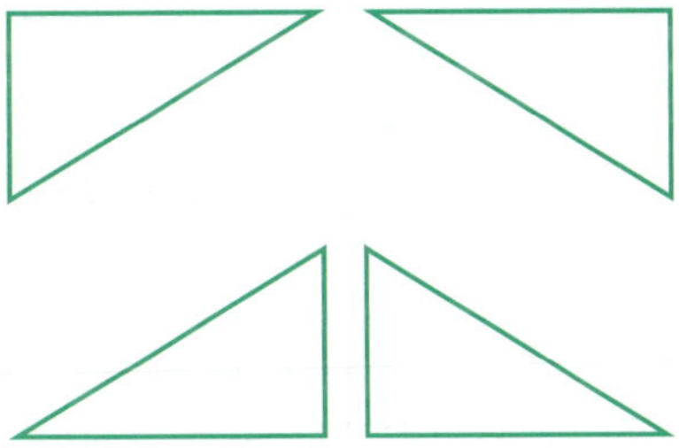

— 1

19 ______ — 1

20 ______

— 1

TOTAL

8

Answers

Maths Test

Question number	Answer	Mark	Parent's notes and additional information
Part A			
1	349 and "three hundred and forty-nine"	1	Accept incorrect spellings where the intention is clear, e.g. "hunded" or "fourty".
2	Ingrid	1	
3	26 = 100 – 74 42 = 14 x 3 57 = 28 + 29 36 = 6 x 6 82 = 68 + 14 59 = (20 x 3) – 1	2	Award one mark if all but two matches are correct.
4a	1, 4, 9, **16,** 25, **36** Both must be correct for a point to be awarded.	1	Children should recognise that these are square numbers. A square number is a number that is made from multiplying another number by itself, e.g. 1 = 1 x 1, 4 = 2 x 2, 9 = 3 x 3… etc. Children should learn the square numbers to 100, i.e. 1, 4, 9, 16, 25, 36, 49, 64, 81,100.
4b	3, 6, 12, **24, 48**, 96	1	Children should notice that this is a doubling pattern.
5a	4	1	
5b	5	1	
5c	3	1	
6	octagon	1	
7		2	**Three** lines should be marked on Badge A, in the places shown. **One** only should be marked on Badge B and **two** on Badge C. A mirror or tracing paper can be used for this question. Award one mark if only two badges are correctly marked.

Question number	Answer	Mark	Parent's notes and additional information
8	23, 18 Only these two should be ringed.	1	Children should recognise patterns in the remainders created by dividing by 5, e.g. 12, 17, 22, 27… all have a remainder of 2 when divided by 5. Similarly, 13, 18, 23, 28… have remainders of 3.
9	18 cm^2	1	Areas of shapes can be found by counting the number of squares (including part squares) inside the shape. Alternatively, this shape can be broken into a square (3 squares by 3 squares = 9 squares) and two triangles, each half the area of a 3 x 3 square.
10	256	1	Children might incorrectly give the answer 16 by dividing rather than multiplying by four.
11a	3 minutes	1	
11b	Floor 4	1	
11c	9.22	1	
12	The pyramid should be ticked. 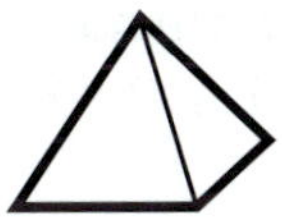	1	A prism is a shape with the same cross-section along its length. It has two identical faces at either end.
13	An explanation that includes reference to numbers such as 1, 4, 9, 16, 25, and/or an explanation of multiplying a number by itself to create a square number, and/or the suggestion that these numbers of dots can be arranged to form a square, e.g. 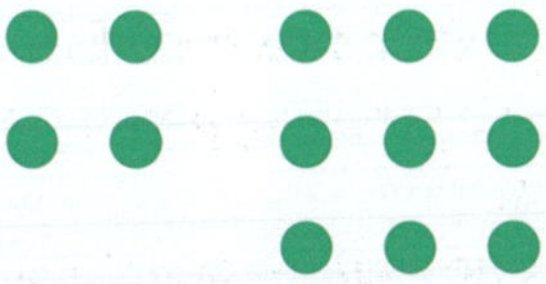	1	A square number is a number that is made from multiplying another number by itself, e.g. 1 = 1 x 1, 4 = 2 x 2, 9 = 3 x 3. Children should learn the square numbers to 100, i.e. 1, 4, 9, 16, 25, 36, 49, 64, 81,100.
14a	74 – **46** = 28	1	

Maths Test Answers

Question number	Answer	Mark	Parent's notes and additional information
14b	**17** + 39 = 56	1	Some children may make the mistake of adding 39 and 56. Children need to realise that despite having an addition sign, this question can be answered by subtracting 39 from 56.
15	$\frac{2}{5}$	1	
16		1	Each of the other shapes does not meet the description in at least one way.
17	53	1	Any non-calculator method can be used to find the answer.
18	800 ml	1	Children need to know that there are 1000 ml in one litre.
19	$6.21 \rightarrow 6$ $5\frac{1}{4} \rightarrow 5$ $7\frac{7}{8} \rightarrow 8$ $6.09 \rightarrow 6$ $7.48 \rightarrow 7$ $5\frac{9}{10} \rightarrow 6$	2	Award two marks for all correct. If at least four of the six are correctly joined, award one mark.
20	$\frac{1}{2}$	1	Children can often become confused with probability questions of this type. Just because a result has occurred once, it is no less likely to happen again the next time. On the second spin there is still a one in two chance of scoring a 2, so the probability must be one-half.
21	A rectangle with the length and the width totalling 22 cm, e.g. 10 cm and 12 cm or 11 cm and 11 cm etc. The angles should be right angles.	1	The perimeter is the distance all the way around the shape. If the perimeter is 44 cm, then the total of the four sides is 44 cm.

Question number	Answer	Mark	Parent's notes and additional information
Part B			
22a	£6000	1	Any non-calculator method is acceptable.
22b	£575	1	To find 15% of £500, children can first find 15% of £100 (=£15) and then multiply this by 5 to find 15% of 500. Alternatively, this can be viewed as $\frac{15}{100}$ x 500 or 15 ÷ 100 x 500.
23	£38.43	1	Any non-calculator method is acceptable.
24	16	1	To find the median, the numbers must be ordered. Once ordered, the median value is the number in the middle of the list, e.g. 3, 11, 12, **16**, 17, 20, 20
25	$\frac{4}{5}$	1	The probability of a card being a number between 3 and 10 inclusive is eight out of ten or four-fifths.
26	48 cubes	1	A common error that children make with this question is to divide 12 by 4 to give the incorrect answer 3. Show your child that the height is always smaller than the number of cubes used to make the model. So if the height is given as 12 cm, it must take more than 12 centimetre cubes to make it.
27a	A = – 0.3	1	
27b	B = 0.7	1	
28a	nine litres	1	72 ÷ 8 = 9
28b	104 miles	1	13 x 8 = 104
29	2 hours 50 minutes	1	If your child has answered 3 hours 10 minutes, show him or her that 3 hours 10 minutes on from 16:35 is 19:45 not 19:25. Javed watches TV for 10 minutes **less** than three hours, not more.
30	5000 paces	1	If each pace is 60 cm, then after five paces she has gone 300 cm (3 m). So after 5000 paces she will have travelled 3000 m, which is the same as 3 km. Children need to know that 1000 m = 1 km.
31	13	1	If *x* stands for the number 3, then five lots of *x* (five lots of 3) must equal 15. 15 – 2 = 13 so ▲ has the same value as 13.
32a	0.3674	1	
32b	54.08	1	

Answers

Mental Maths Test

1. 52
2. 56
3. 6009
4. 30 kg
5. 40 minutes
6. 37
7. 11 m
8. 1205
9. 9 degrees
10. 37
11. 50p
12. Any two numbers that add to make $7\frac{1}{2}$ e.g. $6\frac{1}{2}$ + 1 or 3.2 + 4.3, etc.
13. 1500 g
14. 6
15. $\frac{1}{2}$ or $\frac{3}{6}$
16. £19.95
17. 3.45
18. 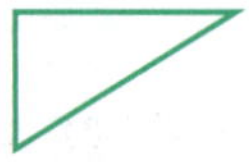
19. 16
20. 30°

Award one mark per correct answer.

The test score is out of a maximum of 45 marks (30 marks for Part A and 15 for Part B).

If your child has scored highly in Part A, he or she should go on to try the harder questions in Part B.

Write your child's scores below:

Mark scored in Part A	28	out of 30
Mark scored in Part B	10	out of 15
Total	38	out of 45

Children at Year 5 may complete a test of this type at school. From this each child can be levelled and graded according to his or her total score. The score for mental maths is not included when levelling at Year 5.

Total marks 45

Mark	0–10	11–15	16–20	21–25	26–30	31–35	36–39	40–45
Level	Below 3	3c	3b	3a	4c	4b	4a	5

Lythiah

If a child scores very highly on the test, there is a possibility of sitting the Year 6 tests, to gain clearer information about the level at which he or she is performing.

English at Year 5

The Year 5 Optional Tests in English cover reading, writing and spelling. Schools do not have to use them, but many do, in order to assess their pupils' progress from one year to the next and to help them to become accustomed to the format of tests.

Levels

Most children attain Level 3 by the end of Year 4; by the end of Year 5 they will be well on the way to Level 4 and may even have attained Level 4. Some might attain Level 5.

You can gain an idea of the approximate level at which your child is working by following the conversion tables on page 58, which show how to convert the marks into a National Curriculum Level. No marks are given for writing, but the chart on page 56 will help you to judge your child's level of attainment.

Setting the test

A relaxed approach is best. If you feel anxious, your child will sense this and might not concentrate or perform as well as he or she could.

Work in a quiet place where you and your child will not be distracted.

Give your child the tests in the order in which they appear in this book. This is important because the tests are linked by a theme. To understand the Writing Test, your child needs to have done the Reading Test.

Your child will need a pencil and, if possible, an eraser; if you do not have an eraser, ask your child to cross out any mistakes made.

No extra paper is needed: your child writes in this book.

Do not ask your child to do all the tests one after the other.

To the side of each question is a number indicating how many marks the question is worth, and a circle in which you enter your child's mark.

After each test, add up your child's marks and use the conversion table on page 58 to work out his or her approximate National Curriculum Level.

Encourage your child and give praise for what he or she can do. Do not dwell on what he or she *cannot* do but, at another time, you could provide practice in the areas where it is needed. Be guided by your child's teacher as to what are the best ways in which you can help.

In this booklet, we shall look at aspects of the Vikings in three different types of of text:

- a fiction text;
- a poem;
- a non-fiction text.

The test is designed to assess your child's ability to read, understand and respond to different types of writing.

Setting the test

Give your child a break between each part of the test.

The overall time allowed for the test is 45 minutes plus 15 minutes for reading the passages (when no writing is allowed). Your child might not need this long.

At the end of the test, enter his or her mark for each question in the circle provided (the number indicates the maximum possible mark).

The answers are on pages 54 to 55.

National Curriculum Levels are given on page 58.

Analysis of previous National Test results in English made the following recommendations, which may be useful during this test:

Reading – Encourage your child to:

- look across the text to see if there are any patterns, e.g. a sequence of events or the use of illustration;
- generalise from two or three instances;
- explain the organisation and layout of texts;
- identify the purpose of the text and the audience for whom it was written;
- explore the precise meaning and effect of words.

Fiction Reading Test

1 Ask your child to turn to the Fiction Reading Test (page 31).

2 Encourage him or her to read the text carefully.

3 Point out that there are two different types of questions: those which give a choice of answers (one of which your child should tick), and those which ask for a written answer. When writing an answer, your child should write in complete sentences, where possible.

4 Do not help your child to read the rest of the text, although you may help with the spelling of the answers. Encourage your child to take care, but point out that he or she may rub out or alter any mistakes made.

5 Ask your child:
- to find the answers in the text, rather than giving answers which he or she already knows;
- to tick only one box to answer each question;
- to try to answer every question;
- to leave any questions he or she cannot answer, and to go back to them at the end;
- to re-read the text to find the answers to any questions which he or she has not answered.

6 Allow your child to write the answers independently after you have helped them. They should use their own words as far as possible unless they are asked to quote from the text.

Poetry Reading Test

Repeat the above for the Poetry Reading Test (page 37).

Non-fiction Reading Test

Repeat the above for the Non-fiction Reading Test (page 40).

From *Egil's Saga*

Egil was restless. He was ready for another sea-voyage. Some years had passed since his raiding expedition to Norway. There had been a furious sea-battle off the coast of Norway, and he had killed Rognvald, the son of King Eirik Bloodaxe, and thirteen of his friends. Eirik declared Egil an outlaw, and his wife, Queen Gunnhild, who was known for her sorcery, put a curse on him.

Egil could not go to Norway – he would be killed at once. But England was surely safe for him – he had fought in a great battle on the side of the king of England, Athelstan: the king owed him a favour. So Egil prepared his ship. In the summer, he left his wife, Asgerd, in charge of their farm at Borg in Iceland, and sailed to England.

He landed on the east coast, not far from York. But he discovered that King Eirik Bloodaxe was there! He had been expelled from Norway and was now king of the Norse people in York. Egil realised that he had no chance of getting away, even in disguise. Someone would recognise him. Besides, he thought it demeaning to be caught trying to run away. So he steeled himself and made up his mind to go to the king.

Egil had a close friend, a Norwegian named Arinbjorn, who was in the service of King Eirik. He went to see Arinbjorn in secret, with some of his crew. Arinbjorn asked him why he had come. Egil told him and said, "Can you give me any help?"

"Did you meet anyone in town who might have recognised you on your way here?" asked Arinbjorn.

"No one," said Egil.

"Then take up your weapons, all of you, and come with me. We must go and see the king," said Arinbjorn.

They set out for the king's residence. The king was sitting at his table. Arinbjorn asked Egil and ten other men to go inside with him.

"Now, Egil," whispered Arinbjorn, "you must offer your head to the king and embrace his foot, and I shall present your case."

They went inside. Arinbjorn went up to the king and greeted him. The king welcomed him and asked what he wanted.

Arinbjorn said, "I have brought here a man who has journeyed a long way to visit you and seek a reconciliation. It is a great honour to you, my lord, when your enemies come to you of their own free will from other lands because they cannot endure your anger even though you are far away. Show this man magnanimity. Make an honourable reconciliation with him for the great honour he does you, by travelling a great distance across difficult seas far from his own home. Nothing but goodwill towards you drove him on this journey."

The king looked around and there, over the heads of the other men, he saw the towering figure of Egil. He glared at him and said, "Why are you so foolhardy, Egil, as to dare to come and visit me? We parted in such a manner last time that you could have no hope of my sparing your life."

Then Egil went up to the table and embraced the king's foot, and spoke a verse of greeting. The king replied, "I need not tally the wrongs you have done me. They are so many and so grave that any one of them would be enough to stop you leaving here alive. You have no hope of anything here but death."

Queen Gunnhild said, "Kill Egil – kill him now! Have you forgotten what he has done? Killed your friends and even your own son, and made you a laughing stock. I have never heard of a king and his family being treated so badly."

Arinbjorn said, "If Egil has done the king wrong he can make up for it with a poem of praise which will live for ever."

Gunnhild said, "We do not want to hear his poem of praise. Have Egil taken outside, Eirik, and put to death at once."

"The king must not let himself be told what to do by you . He must not have Egil killed after nightfall: that would be a shameful act."

The king said, "Let it be as you ask, Arinbjorn. Egil shall live tonight. Take him home with you and bring him to me in the morning."

They went up into the loft in Arinbjorn's house and talked things over. Arinbjorn said, "The king was furious, but seemed to calm down a little. Only luck will decide how things will go. Gunnhild will do her best to have you killed. You must stay up all night and compose a poem in praise of Eirik. You can recite it when we go before him in the morning. That is the only way you might save your head."

Arinbjorn left him. He came back at midnight, and asked him how the poem was going. Egil had not composed a line: "A swallow has been sitting at the window twittering all night and I have not had a moment's peace."

Arinbjorn went up through the door which led to the roof, where the bird had been sitting. He saw a strange shape leaving the house. Arinbjorn sat there outside the window all night until dawn, while Egil composed the poem and memorised it. He recited it to Arinbjorn.

"It is time to go to the king" said Arinbjorn.

Tick the correct answer for questions 1–6.

1 Egil lived in

England	Norway	Iceland	Scotland

1

2 What was the name of Eirik Bloodaxe's son, whom Egil had killed?

Rognvald	Athelstan	Arinbjorn	Eirik

1

3 What stopped Egil from concentrating on composing the poem?

people shouting	a swallow twittering	he was sleepy	a dog barking

1

4 What was the name of King Eirik Bloodaxe's wife?

Gunnhild	Elizabeth	Ethel	Anne

1

5 For which king had Egil fought in England?

Rognvald	Athelstan	Eirik Bloodaxe	Arinbjorn

1

6 Whom did Egil plan to visit when he returned to England?

King Eirik Bloodaxe	King Athelstan	Queen Gunnhild	Arinbjorn

1

TOTAL

6

7 Was Egil tall or short? (1)

How can you tell? (2)

8 How did Egil feel at the beginning of the story? (1)

Why? (1)

9 Why did Egil decide not to try to escape from England? Give two reasons. (2)

10 What reason did Arinbjorn give to King Eirik Bloodaxe for Egil's visit? Give a brief answer. (2)

Was it true? (1)

How can you tell? (2)

TOTAL 12

11 What did King Eirik say should happen to Egil?

1

Why?

1

12 What tells you that Arinbjorn thought King Eirik could be persuaded by flattery?

1

13 Why did King Eirik not kill Egil on the night he went to see him?

1

14 What shows that King Eirik trusted Arinbjorn, even though he was a friend of Egil?

1

15 What did Arinbjorn see when he went to look for the swallow?

1

What do you think it was and who might have sent it?

2

16 What sort of character do you think Gunnhild was?

3

Give two examples from the story to support your answer.

TOTAL

11

1

17 What did Arinbjorn mean by "offer your head to the king"?

1

18 Why did Arinbjorn tell Egil to embrace the king's foot?

1

19 What is sorcery?

3

20 What do you think will happen to Egil?

Why do you think this?

TOTAL

6

A Liking for the Viking

I've always had a liking for the Viking;
His handsome horns;[1] his rough and ready ways;
His rugged russet hair beneath his helmet
In those metal-rattle, battle-happy days.

I've always had a longing for a longboat;
To fly like a dragon through the sea
To peaceful evenings round a real fire,
Alive with legend; rich with poetry.

I've always had a yearning for the burning
Of brave flames irradiating valour;
For the fiery longboat carrying its Chieftain
to his final feast in glorious Valhalla.[2]

Celia Warren

[1] Many pictures of Vikings show them with horned helmets. They wore helmets for battle but these had no horns.
[2] This is the English version of "Valhöll", which means "hall of the slain (killed)".

Tick the correct answer for questions 1–3.

1 What did the writer say Vikings wore on their heads? 1

hoods	helmets	hats	caps

2 Where did they spend their evenings? 1

in bed	in a longboat	in Valhalla	around a fire

3 What is the word for a Viking boat? 1

longboat	dragon	Valhalla	chieftain

4 What do the words "metal-rattle" and "battle-happy" tell you the Viking was like? 1

____

5 What does "valour" mean (verse 3)? 1

____

6 Write an example of a comparison from the poem. 1

____

TOTAL 6

7 Underline the internal rhymes in each of the following lines:

I've always had a liking for a Viking;
I've always had a yearning for the burning

2

8 Underline the examples of alliteration in the following lines:

His handsome horns; his rough and ready ways (2 examples)
His rugged russet hair beneath his helmet (2 examples)

2

9 What contrasts can you find in the second verse?

____

____

____

____

3

10 What do you think the last two lines of the poem are about?

____

____

1

Explain your answer.

____

____

____

1

TOTAL

9

The Jorvik Viking Centre

The Jorvik Viking Centre is unique – once experienced, never forgotten. It is built on the exact site of a huge archaeological dig.

The dig revealed the amazingly well-preserved remains of part of the Viking City of Jorvik from the time of King Eirik Bloodaxe, cocooned in wet mud (and therefore perfectly preserved) for more than 1,000 years. A massive range of detailed, often microscopic, evidence was recovered and has been used to recreate scenes of everyday life. This is no waxworks: this is the closest you'll ever get to time travel – the sights, the sounds and even the very smells of Jorvik in AD 948.

Starting from the moment you arrive at our door, Viking inhabitants of the York of 1,000 years ago will be eager to tell you the best place to buy wooden bowls or bone skates, and tell you about the city in their day, as well as preparing you for your journey back in time. You can dress up as a raider with a sword. Then you descend the stairs to Viking levels – to the level of York's streets as they were in 948 before they were buried beneath the rubbish of subsequent generations.

Climb aboard your magic timecar and then, moving backwards on a journey through time, you will start to move closer and closer to the world of the Vikings in York.

As you emerge from a cordwainer's (shoemaker's) workshop, it is 948 and you are in the bustling market of Coppergate (Coopers' Street) with its mass of traders all shouting for your custom and trying to be heard over all the other noises, of animals, workmen, carts etc. You then turn down one of countless alleys between the houses, workshops and market stalls, and head towards the river. Pick your way past more tradesmen, fighting dogs and scrapping children. You can drive right through a dark, smoky house where a family prepares an evening meal. Herbs, animal skins and furs hang above their heads and foraging chickens cluck around their feet. In the corner children finish spinning and weaving before dinner is ready.

Through the back door and past the squealing piglets, an old chap is sitting on the toilet. Moss and torn-up pieces of old clothes lie on the screen ready for use as toilet paper.

You approach a boat which has just arrived. The sailors sort the cargo, singing songs and cracking a joke or two. Fishermen exchange seafaring yarns, to the delight of a Viking boy who is on fish-gutting duties that evening.

Your journey through time then leaps 1,000 years forwards, as you enter the archaeological excavations upon which the street scene is based. You go through the remains of the house you saw reconstructed.

You leave via the shop, where you can buy books, authentic jewellery and even carved replica bone combs and "Eirik Bloodaxe rules OK" T-shirts! In the coin maker's workshop you can strike a Viking coin using copies of the very moulds found on the site.

Tick the correct answer for questions 1–3.

1 In which city is the Jorvik Viking Centre? 1

the text does not say	York	London	Chester

2 About how long ago was there a Viking settlement at Jorvik? 1

a thousand years	a hundred years	a million years	fifty years

3 What kept the remains of Jorvik in such good condition for all that time? 1

smoke	wet mud	pieces of moss	herbs

4 Which three animals did the people of Jorvik have? 3

____

5 Why are the streets of Jorvik much lower than the modern streets? 1

____

____

6 Name five trades or jobs of adults in Jorvik. 5

____

____

TOTAL 12

7 What three jobs did children do? 3

8 Which two words or phrases are used to create the impression of a busy scene in Coppergate? 2

9 How is the Jorvik Centre different from most museums? 1

10 Which three words or phrases are used to impress this difference upon the reader? 3

11 What kind of audience is addressed by the passage ? 2

How can you tell?

TOTAL

11

12 List any exaggerations or strong adjectives or verbs which are used to show the reader that a visit to the Jorvik Centre will be fun.

____

____

____

3

13 Is the language formal or informal?

____

1

What is it about the person and the form of the verbs which tells you whether the language is formal or informal?

____

____

____

2

Copy a sentence with examples of the verb and person which show this. Underline the verb and person.

____

____

____

2

TOTAL

8

Writing Test

At Key Stage 2 children's writing is assessed through two Writing Tests:

- a Longer Writing Test (45 minutes)
- a Shorter Writing Test (20 minutes).

Children should be allowed time to plan their writing for both tests, which they should not do one after the other.

In the National Tests, the Longer Writing Test is assessed for: **Sentence structure and punctuation**, **Text structure and organisation** and **Composition and effect**. The Shorter Writing Test is assessed for: **Sentence structure, punctuation and text organisation** and **Composition and effect**.

Sentence structure and punctuation focuses on the use of variation of types of sentences, clarity, purpose and effect, and on grammatical accuracy and punctuation.

Text structure and organisation focuses on organising and presenting whole texts effectively, sequencing and structuring information, ideas and events, constructing paragraphs and using cohesion within and between paragraphs.

Composition and effect focuses on imaginative, interesting and thoughtful writing, writing a text which is suitable for its purpose and for the reader, and organising and presenting a text effectively.

Handwriting is assessed in the Longer Test, but it is not assessed in this book.

Spelling is assessed in a separate test.

The mark schemes each year are specific to the tests; new level thresholds are set for each year's tests to ensure that standards are maintained each year.

Assessment of children's attainment in National Tests depends on the judgement of professionals. For the purposes of this book, a simplified system of marking is used based on Content (composition and effect) and Grammar and structure (sentence structure, punctuation and text organisation).

Guidelines to National Curriculum Levels provided on page 56 should be regarded as a rough guide only.

This test helps you to gain an insight into your child's ability to write independently and communicate meaning to the reader using the conventions of punctuation, spelling and handwriting.

Sheets of lined paper are provided on pages 47–48 and 50–51 for your child to write on.

Your child should first have read the passages in the Reading Test.

Allow 45 minutes for the Longer Writing Test and 20 minutes for the Shorter Writing Test.

There are no definitive answers, but criteria are given on page 56 to help you assess your child's Curriculum level.

Longer Writing Test

1. Give your child the planning sheet on page 46.
2. Read the first sentence aloud.
3. Discuss the points on the planning sheet but you must not tell your child what to write!
4. Point out that grammar, spelling and punctuation are important.
5. Remind your child to think about punctuation and how it helps the reader to make sense of what is written.
6. If your child finishes the test before 45 minutes are up, encourage him or her to read it through to look for anything which can be improved and to check grammar, spelling and punctuation.

Shorter Writing Test

1. Give your child the planning sheet on page 49.
2. Read the first sentence aloud.
3. Discuss the points on the planning sheet:
   - writing a whole story in the letter, not just part of it;
   - planning the letter;
   - thinking of a good opening to make the reader want to read on;
   - keeping the reader interested
   - helping the reader to get to know the characters Egil meets;
   - thinking of a good ending, rather than stopping abruptly.

   You must not tell your child what to write!
4. Point out that grammar, spelling and punctuation are important.
5. Remind your child to think about punctuation and how it helps the reader to make sense of what is written.
6. If your child finishes the test before the 20 minutes are up, encourage him or her to read it through to look for anything which can be improved and to check grammar, spelling and punctuation.

Writing Test

Longer Writing Test (Fiction)

Planning sheet

Read *Egil's Saga* (pages 31–32), the poem "A Liking for the Viking" (page 37) and the information passage about the Jorvik Centre (page 40).

Write a newspaper report describing a visit to the Jorvik Centre.

Plan your writing:

- Think about the purpose of your writing.
  Think about the way in which people read newspapers, and where they read them. How will this affect your writing?
  How will you make it easy for someone reading very quickly to gain an impression of the Jorvik Centre?

- Think of a headline.

- Think of other headings.

- Think about the layout of your writing.

Planning sheet

Read *Egil's Saga* (pages 31–32).

Write a letter from Egil to his family at home in Iceland, telling them what happened.

Before you write your letter, you need to plan it.

Make some very brief notes in the spaces below.

- What might have been going through Egil's mind at different points in the story?

- What might he have been thinking about the other characters?

- What words can you use to make the reader want Egil to survive?

- How can you include all the information from the passage?

- What kind of atmosphere do you want to show in the letter, and how will you do that?

Spelling Test

This test contains words which are generally known by ten-year-olds; they include many of the spelling strategies, rules and conventions suggested for Year 5 and the list of high-frequency words for Year 5 in the National Literacy Strategy *Framework for Teaching*.

> This test is a short passage with words missed out.
>
> You read aloud from page 57 (the answers) – copy the text for ease of use. The missing answers are printed in bold.
>
> Your child should write on the test copy on page 53.
>
> Allow 10 minutes for the Spelling Test.
>
> At the end of the test, give a mark for each correct word and enter it in the space provided.
>
> National Curriculum Levels are given on page 58.

1 Ask your child to listen to you reading the complete text.

2 Ask your child to look at his or her copy of the text (page 53). Point out that some of the words have been left out.

3 Tell your child that you are going to read the text again and that he or she should write in the missing words as you read.

4 Read the text aloud again, pausing after each missing word to give your child time to write it on the test copy.

You can repeat each of the missing (bold) words up to three times, if necessary.

Egil was ______________. He was ______________ for ______________ sea-voyage. Some years had ______________ since his ______________ expedition to Norway. There had been a ______________ sea-battle off the coast of Norway, and he had killed Rognvald, the son of King Eirik Bloodaxe, and thirteen of his ______________. Eirik ______________ Egil an outlaw, and his wife, Queen Gunnhild, who was ______________ for her sorcery, put a curse on him.

Egil could not go to Norway – he would be ______________ at once. But England was ______________ safe for him – he had ______________ in a ______________ ______________ on the side of the king of England, Athelstan: the king owed him a ______________. So Egil prepared his ship. In the summer, he left his wife, Asgerd, in ______________ of their farm at Borg in Iceland, and sailed to England.

He landed on the east coast, not far from York. But he ______________ that King Eirik Bloodaxe was there! He had been ______________ from Norway and was now king of the Norse ______________ in York. Egil realised that he had no ______________ of getting away, even in ______________. ______________ would recognise him. Besides, he thought it demeaning to be ______________ trying to run away. So he ______________ himself and made up his mind to go to the king.

TOTAL

24

Answers

Reading Test

Question number	Answer	Mark	Parent's notes and additional information
Fiction Reading Test			
1	Iceland	1	
2	Rognvald	1	
3	a swallow twittering	1	
4	Gunnhild	1	
5	Athelstan	1	
6	King Athelstan	1	
7	Tall. King Eirik could see him above the other men. The phrase "Towering figure".	3	1 mark for each
8	Restless. He had not been on a sea-voyage for a long time.	2	1 mark for each
9	He thought he would be recognised and caught. He would be ashamed to be caught running away.	2	1 mark for each
10	He said that Egil had sailed to England specially to be reconciled with Eirik Bloodaxe. It was not true. Egil planned to visit King Athelstan. He did not know that Eirik Bloodaxe was there, and he wanted to get away from York when he heard that Eirik was there.	2 1 2	
11	He should be killed. Just one of the things he had done was bad enough for him to deserve to die.	2	1 mark for each
12	Arinbjorn tried to persuade him to let Egil live by saying that he would compose "a poem of praise which will live for ever".	1	
13	It was shameful to kill someone at night.	1	
14	He let him take Egil back to his home.	1	
15	A strange shape Something magic *or* something ghostly. It might have been sent by Gunnhild.	3	1 mark for mentioning Gunnhild
16	Evil. She was known for her sorcery. She urged King Eirik to kill Egil.	3	1 mark for each
17	Say that you are giving yourself up to the king's mercy.	1	
18	To show humility/that the king was a great man	1	
19	Witchcraft/casting spells/magic	1	
20	Any answer which is justified by reference to the passage.	3	

Reading Test Answers

Question number	Answer	Mark	Parent's notes and additional information
Poetry Reading Test			
1	helmets	1	
2	around a fire	1	
3	longboat	1	
4	warlike	1	
5	bravery or "being brave"	1	If your child answers "brave" do not allow the mark. Point out that you cannot use "valour" instead of "brave" (e.g. "a brave Viking" but not "a valour Viking").
6	fly like a dragon	1	Discuss what "flies like a dragon" means and the impression this gives of the longboat.
7	liking *and* Viking, yearning *and* burning	2	1 mark for each
8	handsome horns; rough and ready, rugged russet, hair . . . helmet	2	half mark for each
9	"A longboat flying through the sea" is fast and exciting, but "peaceful evenings around a real fire" is calm, quiet and peaceful.	3	Allow three marks for any similar answer.
10	The death of a Viking chieftain. The longboat (in flames) is carrying the chieftain off to the "hall of the killed".	2	Discuss how dead Viking warriors were honoured, and Viking beliefs about death. A Viking chieftain would be burned in his longboat in the belief that this carried him to Valhöll (Valhalla), where Odin, the god of war, gathered his warriors.
Non-fiction Reading Test			
1	York	1	
2	a thousand years	1	
3	wet mud	1	
4	dogs, pigs and chickens	3	1 mark for each
5	Rubbish has piled up on them over the centuries.	1	
6	fisherman, sailor, shoemaker/cordwainer, cooper, coinmaker	5	1 mark for each
7	spinning, weaving, fish-gutting	3	1 mark for each
8	bustling; mass of traders	2	
9	It is built on the exact site of an archaeological dig.	1	
10	unique; once experienced, never forgotten; this is no waxworks	3	
11	Children *or* families. You can dress up as a raider with a sword; magic timecar.	2	
12	unique, huge, massive, microscopic, eager, descend, magic, bustling, countless, scrapping, squealing, etc.	3	
13	Informal. The verbs are active and most of it is in the second person. Any sentence with an active verb in the second person, for example, "You can dress up as a raider".	5	

Answers

Writing Test

The following criteria provide guidelines to help you to gain an idea of your child's Writing Level. Each level assumes that the criteria for the previous level have been met.

Assessment of children's attainment in National Tests depends on the judgement of professionals who use a more precise numerical marking system. For the purpose of this book, a simplified system of marking is used based on Content (composition and effect) and Grammar and structure (sentence structure, punctuation and text organisation).

Content (composition and effect)	**Level**
Do the words and phrases communicate meaning? Does the narrative make sense to the reader?	Level 2
Is the narrative in the correct form (for example, in an appropriate layout and in the correct person and tense)? Is fiction writing imaginative? Is non-fiction writing clear and does it have a logical structure?	Level 3
Is there an attempt to interest the reader? Is the style maintained throughout most of the writing? Are the criteria suggested on the planning sheet met?	Level 4
Is the tone of the writing maintained throughout? Is the language expressive? Does the child make some use of vocabulary which is particularly appropriate (for example, technical language)?	Towards Level 5
Grammar and structure (sentence structure, punctuation and text organisation)	
Are ideas sequenced, with some sentences having capital letters and full stops?	Level 2
Are the ideas presented in sequence, with full stops, capital letters, question marks and commas usually used correctly? Is a greater range of connective words and phrases used (for example, *next*, *afterwards*, *so*)?	Level 3
Are some of the sentences long, with correctly-used connective words and phrases used (for example, *meanwhile*, *however*, *which*, *that*, *who*)? Are conditionals, such as *if* or *because*, used? Do some sentences contain more than one verb or include commas, semi-colons, exclamation marks or speech marks? Are the tense and person consistent throughout? Does the structure of the text add to its effect?	Level 4
Are commas and speech marks used correctly throughout? Is a range of connective words and phrases used? Are punctuation marks used correctly, including brackets or dashes and colons, to separate parts of a sentence? Do the sentences differ in length to express meaning?	Towards Level 5

Egil was **restless**. He was **ready** for **another** sea-voyage. Some years had **passed** since his **raiding** expedition to Norway. There had been a **furious** sea-battle off the coast of Norway, and he had killed Rognvald, the son of King Eirik Bloodaxe, and thirteen of his **friends**. Eirik **declared** Egil an outlaw, and his wife, Queen Gunnhild, who was **known** for her sorcery, put a curse on him.

Egil could not go to Norway – he would be **killed** at once. But England was **surely** safe for him – he had **fought** in a **great battle** on the side of the king of England, Athelstan: the king owed him a **favour**. So Egil prepared his ship. In the summer, he left his wife, Asgerd, in **charge** of their farm at Borg in Iceland, and sailed to England.

He landed on the east coast, not far from York. But he **discovered** that King Eirik Bloodaxe was there! He had been **expelled** from Norway and was now king of the Norse **people** in York. Egil realised that he had no **chance** of getting away, even in **disguise**. **Someone** would recognise him. Besides, he thought it demeaning to be **caught** trying to run away. So he **steeled** himself and made up his mind to go to the king.

Award one mark per correct word.
24 marks in total

National Curriculum Levels

English

Use the conversion tables below to gain an idea of your child's National Curriculum Level.

Fiction Reading		Poetry Reading	
Mark	**Level**	**Mark**	**Level**
0–7	Below 2	0–1	Below 2
8–14	2	2–3	2
15–24	3	4–9	3
25–32	4	10–13	4
33–35	Approaching 5	14–15	Approaching 5

Non-fiction Reading		Spelling	
Mark	**Level**	**Mark**	**Level**
0–5	Below 2	0–1	Below 2
6–11	2	2–4	2
12–21	3	5–13	3
22–28	4	14–20	4
29–31	Approaching 5	21–24	Approaching 5

Total marks

Write your child's marks here:

Non-fiction Reading	
Fiction Reading	
Poetry Reading	
Spelling	
Total (maximum 105)	

Approximate National Curriculum Levels for Reading and Spelling

Marks	0–17	18–35	36–70	71–96	97–105
Level	Below 2	2	3	4	Approaching 5

Notes